KAWASAKI
Z1

ROD KER

AMBERLEY

First published 2016

Amberley Publishing
The Hill, Stroud,
Gloucestershire, GL5 4EP

www.amberley-books.com

ISBN: 978 1 4456 5128 6 (print)
ISBN: 978 1 4456 5129 3 (ebook)

British Library Cataloguing in Publication Data.
A catalogue record for this book is available from the British Library.

Typeset in 10pt on 13pt Celeste.
Typesetting by Amberley Publishing.
Printed in the UK.

Contents

Introduction

The Kawasaki Z1 became a sensation after its launch in 1972, offering incredible performance coupled with convenience, reliability and practicality. While the 1969 Honda CB750 Four is generally accepted as the world's first 'superbike', Kawasaki's 130 mph riposte immediately relegated it to the motorcycling second division, along with Suzuki and Yamaha's contemporary efforts. Meanwhile, the once-unassailable British bike industry was sliding into terminal decline, increasingly unable to compete with Japanese technology and modern manufacturing processes.

Strangely, having leapfrogged the opposition, Kawasaki seemed content to rest on its corporate laurels for many years. Although the Z1 gained capacity and was updated in detail, by the second half of the 1970s it had been 'out-supered' by a wave of new designs from both the Far East and Europe.

However, after a series of essentially cosmetic revisions, the 1980s heralded a complete makeover. The rather lumbering Z1000 was reborn as the fuel-injected GPz1100, its near 150 mph top speed briefly reclaiming the 'Fastest Production Motorcycle' title.

In 1983 Kawasaki went back to the drawing board again and created the all-new, water-cooled GPZ900R, spearheading a future generation of faster, lighter, more efficient hyperbikes, but the essence of the Z1 lived on as the basis for various new models well into the 1990s.

Interestingly, the original Z1 had been dubbed 'classic' years before the term became so overused that its true meaning was lost, so it was only right that it should be the first Japanese motorcycle to become an appreciating asset. Values have risen steadily in the twenty-first century, which might in itself be a good enough reason to buy one. Beyond that, some forty-four years on, King Zed is still great fun to ride and eminently suitable for daily transport.

'Let the Good Times Roll', as the ads used to say.

1

Background

It may seem odd, but you can thank Honda for the existence of the Kawasaki Z1, or Super Four Model Z-1, to use its full original name. The hows and whys are complicated and can be traced back to the immediate post-war period, when Japan was struggling to emerge from devastation and bankruptcy. In the first few decades of the twentieth century, there had been scores of Far Eastern motorcycle marques, but very few of those reappeared after the Second World War. Much of Japan's industry and infrastructure had been obliterated, so there was little chance of a swift reversion to peacetime productivity.

The Tokai Seiki Heavy Industry Company had suffered greatly from bombing. Not a familiar name, perhaps, but most people have heard of its founder, one Soichiro Honda. After an uncharacteristic spell of inactivity, apparently doing little except survey the rubble of his former business and drink homebrew sake, in 1946, at the age of forty, Soichiro set up shop in a glorified wooden shed. Trading under the grand name of the Technical Research Institute, the company mission wavered in the early stages. After a few false starts, Honda realised that what Japan needed most was basic transport to mobilise the masses. Any mode of travel less taxing than walking would be welcome.

The first effort was a moped, or *phut, phut*, in Japanese parlance; a pedal cycle powered by a military surplus two-stroke engine bolted to the frame. When supplies of those ran out, Honda created his own motor, with mixed success. While it has since became apparent that the design was novel and had much potential, in practice it didn't work very well with the available fuels, which tended to be based on turpentine.

However, the re-christened Honda Motor Company's boss was convinced that four-stroke engines were the future, being generally cleaner, more sophisticated and having an attractive exhaust note. He was right! Blazing a trail for the rest to follow, Honda's first four-stroke was a 5 bhp, 146cc overhead valve single, as fitted to the E-Type (not to be confused with a later Jaguar sportscar of the same name). Twin inlet valves were a notable feature, an idea resurrected in the Civic cars and Dream twins of the seventies.

Unfortunately, renewed financial instability in Japan during the early 1950s meant that sophistication was unaffordable for the majority. While Honda was in crisis, other Japanese manufacturers entered the fray, led by Suzuki and Yamaha, both long-established companies diversifying into new markets. The Suzuki Motor Company was an offshoot of the Suzuki Loom Manufacturing Company. Next came Nippon Ghaki, originally founded by Torakusu Yamaha to make musical instruments – hence the three tuning forks emblem. To add further confusion for bike spotters in the future, early Suzukis were badged as Colledas, although a subtle 'S' on the petrol tank gave the game away.

Thanks to the Mitsubishi Bank, by 1955 Honda was firmly on track, literally and figuratively, making bold plans to take on the rest of the world at the Isle of Man TT. That happened before the decade ended, by which time the road bikes had progressed greatly, as exemplified by the C70, a high-revving, 246cc OHC twin with performance equal to that of many 500s.

While the jingoistic element muttered that Honda had simply copied the German NSU Max, that wasn't fair. In the years that followed, the Japanese became the innovators, not the imitators, and Honda's 'four-stroke only' policy proved increasingly far-sighted. Despite its rather rotund and dumpy appearance, the C70 could be seen as the root of all Honda's greatest hits, including the 750 Four, which in turn inspired, or obliged, competitors to produce bikes in the same mould, unflatteringly known as Universal Japanese Motorcycles.

Soichiro Honda, the most significant figure in the post-Second World War Japanese motorcycle industry. (Courtesy of Honda)

KHI WORLD

While today Kawasaki Heavy Industries has 31 major manufacturing plants (including 13 outside Japan) it still remains an engineer's company – with engineers well represented in senior management – just as it did when founded in 1878. Consequently, all the products are designed to deliver the best possible combination of performance, reliability and efficiency.

Quite apart from its sister companies – Kawasaki Shipping Line and Kawasaki Steel Corporation – which operate as autonomous industrial groups, KHI's operations are now divided into seven major categories:

Aircraft This group produces complete fixed wing aircraft, helicopters and missiles, as well as major aircraft components –such as the fuselage of the new Boeing 767. Some of this work is in conjunction with, or under licence from, other major aircraft companies such as Lockheed, Boeing, Hughes and Messerschmitt-Bolkow-Blohm GmbH.

Energy Plant Engineering Designs and builds such major components for thermal and nuclear power plants as high-pressure boilers and heat exchangers. Also large scale solar energy systems and geothermal powerplants.

Engines and Motorcycles Produces a full range of motorcycles from 50-1300cc. Also diesel and petrol engines, jet and gas turbines plus gears, transmissions and generators.

Machinery Designs and builds computer controlled robots and hydraulic equipment for industrial use. Also air compressors, gas compression modules, blowers, variable-pitch propellers, wear-resistant steels and heavy construction machinery.

Plant Engineering Designs and builds major plants for production of steel, cement, chemicals and liquified nitrogen gas. Also constructs major high-rise building frames, bridges and storage tanks.

Rolling Stock Passenger carriages, locomotives, freight cars, underground railways and mono rails. Also cable car systems and fully automated transit systems.

Ships Designs and builds major vessels for transport of crude oil, liquified gas, containers, cars, refrigerated and general cargo. Other vessels include icebreakers, submarines, patrol and research boats plus marine based industrial plant. Also constructs drilling platforms and self elevating platforms for undersea construction work.

Naturally, with such diverse operations under one roof, KHI has a vast store of engineering expertise and advanced technology. One of the world's largest R&D programmes ensures that ALL divisions benefit from new advances, helping keep each a leader in its field.

Examples? Aircraft research has given all

divisions the latest data on lightweight, high strength metal alloys and synthetic materials. R&D on powerplants ranging from oil tanker engines to sub-compact car engines provides the technology on every aspect of internal combustion engines, while continuing development on computer control systems provides up-to-date electronics technology.

While other manufacturers have explored a wide variety of designs and market concepts, Kawasaki prefers to remain faithful to carefully selected basic designs, refining each to the limit of its potential. The result has been Kawasaki consistently setting leading standards for peak performance and reliability – making these attributes virtually company trademarks.

Top right, solar heating for a warehouse. Top, Kawasaki built BK117 helicopter, with Kawasaki Unimate industrial robots in action below. Next is just one example of heavy construction machinery produced, while at bottom is a liquified nitrogen gas container ship. Above right is a cement manufacturing plant, while below that is the famous 'Bullet' high speed train, yet another Kawasaki product.

Without Honda's trailblazing, Suzuki, Yamaha and Kawasaki Heavy Industries would probably never have diversified into two-wheeled transport after the Second World War.

9

2

Enter Kawasaki

By a slightly scenic route, this brings us to Kawasaki, the last of the Japanese Big Four tank badges to emerge. A vast conglomerate manufacturing virtually everything, trains, boats and planes included, the motorcycle connection surfaced in 1952 with the KE-1 engine, a 148cc four-stroke single, designed by the aircraft division. Like the British Villiers company, Kawasaki was content to supply engines to house other manufacturers' chassis, including Meihatsu and the long-established Meguro concern.

It's interesting to note that Kawasaki produced a 150cc four-stroke at almost the same time as Honda, only to abandon it in favour of two-strokes for about twenty years. What might have been! Instead, 1955 gave us the KB-5, a German DKW 125-esque two-stroke single (as were the BSA Bantam and Harley-Davidson Hummer, appropriated as war reparations) that in improved 'A' guise powered the dull but dependable Meihatsu 125 commuter.

Kawasaki finally came out of the corporate closet the following year, when the manufacturer's name was stamped into the engine side covers for the first time. It then made sense for them to make the whole motorcycle. To this end, Meguro was absorbed by the aircraft division and Kawasaki Auto Sales was set up in Tokyo. With a new factory dedicated exclusively to motorcycle production, the first complete bikes to be branded as Kawasakis (the tank badge actually said 'Kawasaki Aircraft') were the 125 New Ace, 125B7 and 125B8: small names for unassuming 125cc two-stroke runabouts. Truly a modest start for a company with such huge resources.

If the small-scale start was puzzling, the next step might seem baffling at first sight, as Kawasaki decided to enter the world of Japanese motocross racing with the B8M. This was followed by the curiously monikered Red Tank Furore (yes, it had a red petrol tank), which won most races and had a fearsome reputation.

To progress, the company development path had to embrace larger-capacity machines and an assault on America, by far the largest market for bikes in the sport and leisure field. This came to fruition in 1966 with the A1 Samurai, a 250cc twin two-stroke with the novelty of rotary valve induction. The A7 Avenger, an expanded version, nominally a 350 but actually a 320, arrived soon after. Rounding up capacities has long been accepted practice in motorcycling! Both these twins were high performers, the 250 having 30 bhp and the A7 40 bhp, good for well over 100 mph.

Samurai 250 and Avenger 350 twins were Kawasaki's first larger-capacity bikes.

In the same year, Kawasaki also launched the W1, a 624cc, OHV twin, at the time the largest capacity Japanese-made motorcycle. This was actually an expanded and updated version of the old Meguro 500 K-series, which was effectively a replica of the ancient BSA A7 / A10, a defunct model abandoned by BSA in 1962 in favour of the unitary construction A50/65 twins. Not likely to sell in the patriotic UK, but, again, the method in Kawasaki's apparent madness was that the US was the main outlet for large-capacity bikes. Americans loved British parallel twins almost as much as they loved their home-grown V-twin hogs, so launching the W1 gave Kawasaki instant presence, preparing us for what came next.

What might have come next was a four-cylinder, four-stroke 750cc motorcycle with twin overhead camshafts. Development began at Akashi in 1967, and everything was going to plan, only for Honda to spoil everything by launching the CB750 in autumn 1968, at about the same time as Kawasaki's prototype was nearing completion. After due consideration, and no doubt much gnashing of teeth, it was decided that there would be no point in producing a bike so similar to the Honda Four. Development team leader Sam Tanegashima had to shelve what was at that stage known as project N600.

In the meantime, Kawasaki ditched the two-stroke twins and finished work on a concurrent project in the form of the infamous two-stroke triples. Starting in 1969 with the H1 500, variations on the theme in 250, 350, 400 and 750cc capacities were later produced. Forthcoming US emissions regulations gave these celebrated 'Green Meanies' a limited life expectancy in any case (the same applying to their riders, sadly) so Kawasaki had to have a clean alternative ASAP, although naturally it was also important that the new bike wasn't rushed into production. It has been suggested that Honda did exactly that with the CB750, a machine everyone craved in 1969 but few could actually buy for a year, simply due to lack of supply.

Infamous 'Green Meanie' (note, not always green!) triples, launched in 1969.

First seen as the Mach III 500, this is the later, slightly tamed version.

500 triple was followed up by 750, 250, 350 and 400 models, all with unique sound, fury and ridiculous petrol consumption.

Mach IV 750 was actually less of a handful to ride than the original wild 500.

Left: CB450 twin, Honda's ultimate until the CB750 Four.

Below: Launched in late 1968, Honda's CB750 caused Kawasaki to shelve what later became the Z1.

3

The Superbike Seventies

As the acknowledged world's first 'superbike', Honda's CB750 had a market to itself as the 1970s dawned. Production problems and a few technical issues had been addressed, so the Four was deservedly selling like proverbial hotcakes. Unhappily for the traditional industry, sales came mainly at the expense of big Harley-Davidsons and British bikes, particularly the Triumph Trident and BSA Rocket 3, which had beaten Honda to the market, but lacked the pizzazz (as the contemporary argot had it), while still relying on old technology.

BSA-Triumph's three-cylinder engine was very much based on the Speed Twin, which could trace its origins back to 1937. Then there was the Norton Commando 750, also powered by an ancient engine that first saw the light of day as a 500 before being enlarged to 600cc, 650cc then 750cc. That wasn't the end, though, because the Commando subsequently became an '850' (828cc in reality). Incredibly, the same engine has since been expanded to displace a full litre, but that's another story.

It must have been mystifying and possibly embarrassing for Honda to find that the quaint old Commando 750 was as fast as the CB750. The problem was that in achieving these feats the Norton was stressed to the limit, while the Four was in a mild state of tune and running well within its capabilities. To put another nail in the coffin, features like a disc brake, five-speed gearbox and electric starter were still several years away for British bikes, when the battle had already been lost.

Unfortunately, in the absence of serious investment in new machine tools and modern factories, the rest of the world couldn't copy Japan, even if they wanted to. As the 1960s turned into the 1970s, the British in particular struggled on with primitive methods, with often little changed since the 1930s. To illustrate the point, it was reported that when Velocette went out of business, parts of its Birmingham base still relied on candles for lighting!

And all British bikes leaked oil, of course. In contrast, precision machining, die casting and horizontally split crankcases meant that Japanese bikes rarely allowed lubricant that should have stayed inside the engine to reach the outside world. Yet, as anyone who'd been in the vicinity of one of the two-stroke triples could confirm, oil poured out of their exhausts, along with a lethal cocktail of atmospheric pollutants. So when Kawasaki resurrected the four-cylinder project for 1970, chief engine designer Ben Inamura had far more obstacles to face than had been the case in the simple sixties, when petrol was used as a coolant as well as a fuel and California was only just beginning to disappear in a toxic haze.

Left: Heading into the 1970s, BSA's swansong 650, promoted by one of the most honest slogans ever.

Below: Suzuki's GT750 three-cylinder was flawed when it arrived, but subsequently became one of the most endearing and enduring superbikes.

Above: Yamaha XS1, XS2 and XS650 were effectively modernised versions of British big twins. (Courtesy of Yamaha)

Right: Against all the odds, Norton's 750 and 850 Commandos were as fast as anything with two wheels before the Z1 arrived.

BMW began the 1970s with some very staid models. That changed dramatically with the R90S.

Triumph Bonneville in slightly ungainly T140 trim sold well once the factory sit-in was over.

Bike British. You've arrived.

Remember what it felt like when you bought your first bike? It felt good. It felt like you'd arrived and everybody knew it.

Well that's what it feels like to own a Big British Bike.

Suddenly, you find yourself with a reputation to keep up. You start to go places you didn't go before. Meet people you never knew before.

It's the kind of reputation that stems from the bikes themselves.

Nortons and Triumphs. Bikes that handle like nothing else on the road. Race-bred bikes that get you where you want to go. Fast. Safe.

If you think you can handle this kind of reputation, see your Norton Triumph dealer and talk yourself into a Big British Bike.

Do it now. And you'll know you've arrived.

Norton Triumph

Norton Triumph Europe Limited, Andover, Hants.

Win a British Superbike!

OVER £3,000 WORTH OF PRIZES TO BE WON.

Order a Triumph or a Norton before 31st December 1974 and you could win another one free!

That's the offer we're making you if you order your bike before the end of October, November, or December, as we're giving away one bike every month.

When you order, you'll get a competition entry form – **the chance to win another Norton or Triumph of your own choice absolutely free.** And even if you don't win, you'll still receive tickets for 1975 Transatlantic Match Races when you take delivery of your Triumph or Norton. So you can't lose.

See your local dealer for full details.

BIKE BRITISH BONANZA

Casual racism from Norton Triumph's 1974 ads.

4

Heavy Engineering

Unmistakable: the Super 4 Model Z-1, as launched in 1972.

While Honda had unhelpfully moved the goalposts, Kawasaki's riposte, known to insiders as project New York Steak, was going to be similar in general terms, if very different in detail. Yes, both featured a transverse, four-cylinder engine, but Inamura could never have been accused of copying the CB750. At a glance, it was obvious the Kawasaki had two overhead camshafts. Honda had already tried that in 1965 with the CB450 twin, but for whatever reason had reverted to a single cam for the Four, and the new K-series twins released at the same time. Perhaps it was considered unnecessary for an engine producing 90 bhp per litre? Possibly it was to reduce weight, size and complication?

According to Kawasaki, 'DOHC was necessary to realise overall high performance from low speed to high speed range. In motorcycle markets around the world, there were only one or two other examples of this type of engine, and it was the first engine for Kawasaki to adopt this advanced valve train.' Allowing for losses in translation, this doesn't really mean much. It's hard not to suspect that oneupmanship and style were the motives.

To recap on the Honda Four's engine layout, it had dry sump lubrication, pressure feeding a one-piece crankshaft running in split shell bearings. Of undersquare (aka long stroke) configuration, the camshaft turned in two separate carriers incorporating plain bearings on top of the cylinder head, driven by a central sprocket and roller chain. The valves were opened by rockers, with screw adjustment for tappet clearance accessible through eight screw-fit covers.

Another pair of sprockets alongside the one driving the cam took power through a pair of roller chains to a multiplate clutch and five-speed gearbox. Moving rearwards, an extra geared shaft finally drove the outboard secondary chain. Most motorcycle engines with chain drive do without the extra transmission stage.

That includes the Z1, in which the secondary gearbox shaft drove the rear chain directly. Kawasaki's crankcases were shorter as a result, with the additional benefit of potentially reducing power loss, mechanical noise and backlash. Part of the reason Mr Inamura could do this was that, upstream of the Z1's massive 8-plate clutch, primary drive was by means

Bubblewrapped for posterity.

The first model, distinguished by bold yellow or orange tank panels and black main engine cases.

Z1 and Z1A side panel badges. The Z1B and Z900 are different.

Neat underseat arrangement. The air intake is prone to obstruction.

of gears, rather than Honda's pair of roller chains, which gave one less reversal of rotation. The alternative would have been to have the crankshaft running 'backwards' (i.e. in opposite direction to the wheels), which can in theory affect handling, although in practice it probably makes little difference when weighed against the other multitude of influences.

In fact, Kawasaki's next four-stroke, the 1974 Z400 twin, did have chain primary drive and a backwards engine, but, alas, poor handling was the least of its problems! Two years later the Z650 four adopted a completely different layout by introducing a jackshaft between the crankshaft and clutch/gearbox, driven by an inverted tooth chain in this case. With one more change of drive direction, the engine could run 'forwards' and made better use of space. Ben Inamura again headed the Z650 design team, but the jackshaft concept had first appeared on Honda's second four, the often-overlooked CB500 that appeared in 1971. More 'transfer engineering'? Possibly, but the Z650 did have a double overhead cam top end like the Z1.

As with the three-cylinder two-strokes, King Zed's crankshaft was a built up assembly, pressed together complete with rolling element bearings for the mains and big ends. While being more expensive and noisier than plain bearings, the six-caged roller bottom end was incredibly strong and only needed a trickle of oil to survive (at 2.8 psi, according to the blurb), as was proved in later years, when basically the same engine was producing around 20 per cent more power. In contrast, starved of high-pressure lubrication, plain bearings will be wrecked in seconds.

Moving upwards past the one-piece con-rods, various guides and jockey wheels that kept the long cam chain under control, we reach the cylinder head. Essentially a single casting, despite those twin camshafts, the Z1 top end was actually more simple than the SOHC CB750's, with its extra layer of rocker gear and bearings. The Zed's cams sit in four plain bearings that have the welcome refinement of separately replaceable shells, so a lubrication disaster, for whatever reason, won't destroy the entire head.

The top end was a novelty in production motorcycles, if not in the car world, where Jaguar for one had been selling twin-cam XK engines with directly actuated valves since 1948. Alfa Romeo, Fiat and even Ford had followed. Instead of rockers pushing open the valves, the Z1's cam lobes lived just above the tappets (commonly referred to as buckets), with lash set by interposed shims of varied thickness. Because the shims and buckets tended to turn round as they were wiped by the lobes, wear was minimal, so adjustment for that reason was a rare event. Unfortunately, any recession of the valve seat would reduce the tappet gap, and eventually the valve would be held open slightly, causing a vicious circle of wear. Old-time Jaguar mechanics knew that totally silent valve gear heralded trouble, but Kawasaki fitted super-hard sintered seats to cope with unleaded fuel, so recession wasn't a problem.

ND speedometer calibrated only at 20 mph intervals. The orifice to the right is supposedly to hold the ignition key when not in use!

Stamping on exhaust alluding to both 900 and Japanese market Z2 750.

The main technical justification for using cams directly pushing open the valves is to reduce reciprocating weight, thereby avoiding float while potentially increasing maximum revs (or allowing use of softer springs). In reality, the advantage is less clear cut because with rocker-arm valve gear not all the mass between the cam lobe and valve is actually reciprocating. Musing further on the pros and cons of DOHC, the extra bulk and weight, concentrated high up, is certainly not a help in either car or motorcycle applications. It's worth remembering that Mr Honda demonstrated in the 1978 CX500 that a well-designed OHV twin could rev happily to 10,000 rpm without valve control problems.

In Jaguar's case, the rev ceiling was far more likely to be set by its long stroke. Perhaps equally important, the XK engine looked magnificent, which was paramount in an era when enthusiasts delighted in opening the bonnet with a flourish. It's likely true to say that Jaguars with less aesthetically pleasing engines would have been less successful, even if they'd had more performance! Their founder, Sir William Lyons, definitely understood marketing.

So did Kawasaki, because in those days motorcycle engines were permanently on show, as fairings were completely out of fashion, except for the occasional Triumph Saint or Norton Interpol police bike. BMW began to reverse the trend with the 90S and 100RS, but ironically it was Kawasaki's GPZ900R of 1983 that made fairings almost obligatory on anything but cruisers. As a consequence, for three decades sports-bike engines have been largely water-cooled and out of sight – if not mind – as it would be hard not to be aware of 200 bhp at 11,000 rpm.

Kawazaki's trademark ducktail. The rounded rear lamp on Z1/A/B changed for more rectangular style on the Z900.

To return to the hot topic of the early 1970s – emissions control – there was some mystery about the purpose of the round appendage lurking under the Z1's quartet of 28-mm Mikuni carburettors. Honda put the Four's oil filter in a finned casting poking out of the front of the crankcases, so it might have been assumed that this was a variation on the theme. In fact, the filter was in the sump and the alloy appendage behind the barrels was part of the Positive Crankcase Ventilation system, which involved feeding crankcase fumes back to the intake side through a separator, rather than simply releasing the engine's bad breath into the atmosphere. Hey presto, a 40 per cent reduction in hydrocarbon emissions. Cars had used similar devices for years, so it wasn't a new idea. Slightly ironically, going back to 1957, Triumph's new unit 350 twin featured a timed breather that doubled as a chain oiler, but later models went back to basics.

Before the launch, Honda's Four had been rumoured to produce 100 bhp at incredible revs, just like the race bikes. From 736cc, the reality turned out to be 67 bhp at 8000 rpm and a fairly mild state of tune. Apparently for no other reason other than to set it apart from 'a competitor' (as Kawasaki literature coyly acknowledges Honda, the world's largest motorcycle manufacturer!), New York Steak was beefed up from the opposition's three-quarter litres. Seemingly without concern for established engine sizes, the Z1 had 'square' 66-mm dimensions, giving 903cc. With an extra 167cc over Honda, claimed power was 82 PS (around 81 bhp) at 8500 rpm, so it was very close in specific output.

While it was accepted that Kawasaki had come up with a masterpiece when it was introduced to the public in September 1972, evidently there were plenty of issues to be

Most of King Zed's engine top end. Generally easy to work on.

sorted out during development, so it's fortunate that the gestation period was about twice as long as normal. Perish the thought: in the prototype stage, piston collapses, oil leaks and crankshaft breakages have been mentioned.

Apart from concentrating market research in the USA, American journalists were drafted in to work with Kawasaki, both in Japan and during final development on Uncle Sam's side of the Pacific. In 1971, Bryon Farnsworth from *Cycle* magazine was appointed senior test rider and was invited to tell it like it was, with strict instructions not to be polite! (With hindsight, we can see that the rather cosy and deferential attitude of the British press to home-grown products contributed to the downfall of the once all-powerful industry.) Then, in early 1972, the ultimate prototypes were shipped to America to roam the roads in press hands, thinly disguised as Hondas. The all-star factory race team, which included British rider Paul Smart and Gary Nixon, also joined the fun, basically riding flat out on road and track for as long as possible in an effort to expose any weaknesses.

A coast-to-coast magical mystery tour of America, clocking around 5,000 miles and taking in Los Angeles and Daytona Beach, established that the engine was brilliant. But contemporary tyres and chains couldn't stand the pace. 5,000 miles was easily far enough to vaporise a couple of rear boots and the heavy-duty drive chain, despite Kawasaki's thoughtful provision of a pumped oil feed. Honda had also initially provided automatic oiling on the Honda CB750, but technology only really caught up a few years later when O-ring chains with sealed in lubricant became available.

The 'King of Motorcycles' wasn't just an engine, though. Kawasaki was determined to make the Z1 a complete package, so the chassis was more than an afterthought, as had been a criticism of the fearsome two-stroke triples. Sticking to the historic general pattern of the Norton 'featherbed', the frame was a double loop cradle with much bracing around the steering head – similar to the Honda Four's, in most respects, although Kawasaki had contrived to leave enough room to remove the entire top end without disturbing the lower half of the engine. Hopefully that wouldn't be necessary for the next 100,000 miles, but it showed that the Z1 wasn't going to be an impractical, disposable item.

Moving back, the Zed had a waspish waist, helping to make it look less bulbous than the Honda opposition, even though it was actually bigger. The compact appearance and unthreatening seat height was at least partly due to the Z1 carrying its oil in the sump, so there was no problem with finding room for a gallon tank and associated plumbing, as with the dry-sump CB750.

One Honda oddity was the square-section swinging arm made of welded pressings. Kawasaki remained faithful to round tube throughout. From the steering head backwards, the chassis looked strong, but the front end seemed slightly less inspiring, because the fork sliders were very short, leaving a long expanse of spindly 36-mm stanchion to twist and flex. Appearances can sometimes be deceptive, though ...

DOHC engine's lower half reassembly after cleaning. Cylinder head studs will probably be heavily corroded and seized to barrels. Make sure oilways on outer rear studs are clear!

5

Reign in California

Apart from being deeply involved with development, American magazines based in smoggy California, close to the US importers, were naturally the first to publish tests. Late in 1972 *Cycle Guide* gushed:

> The Kawasaki 903 Z1 is the most modern motorcycle in the world. It is also the fastest. It is above all the first of a new generation of bikes, a generation which will run quietly on the streets of America, a generation which will attempt to solve motorcycles' tiny contribution to the world's dirty air; it is the first of a generation of motorcycles which will come close to being within reason all things to all people, capable of nattering down quiet country roads packing double one minute and rotating the Earth with incomprehensible acceleration the next.

Rotating the Earth with 81 bhp seemed slightly optimistic (or pessimistic), but a standing quarter mile in under 12.5 seconds and a top speed of around 135 mph were still impressive figures. Deadly rival *Cycle* also waxed lyrical in describing the riding experience: 'Horsepower flows like water from an Artesian well. It simply never stops.'

Cycle Guide continued: 'The thing that impresses you about the 900 is its great straight-line stability at very high speeds. We could cruise at 120 mph sitting bolt upright.' Sounds like the perfect motorcycle, then? Without wishing to cast aspersions, when the Z1 finally arrived in Europe, not everyone was convinced about the stability. In fact, King Zed soon gained a reputation for being almost as handlebar happy as the infamous Green Meanies, although there were others who didn't have any trouble.

It sounds silly, but these differing perceptions probably had much to do with riding style. Fast means very different things to different people. Any bike with an upright riding position and huge cowhorn handlebars will also be unduly affected by the wind and road surface. So, while 120 mph cruising may have felt fine on a still day on a deserted, dry American interstate, the same feat on a cracked section of M1 concrete on a breezy day, surrounded by rampant lorries and Ford Cortinas, is another matter entirely. In the wrong conditions, with the wrong rider, weaving, wobbling and even tank-slappers were possibilities.

Above: Also available in yellow.

Left: Double-cradle frame looks very strong around steering head, but cracking around gusset plates is not unknown.

As with the Honda Four, chain wear was a major problem until the O-ring variety appeared later in the 1970s.

Apart from the human parachute riding position and rearward weight distribution (ever more so with increasing speed), many bikes of the era suffered from having narrow wheels and less-than-ideal tyres. One of the exceptions was the Triumph Trident T150, which came with a set of the latest 'trigonal' profile Dunlop TT100s as standard. Aside from whatever clever rubber compound they were made of, they had lower aspect ratios, helping to reduce flex. The TT100, aka K81, was developed specifically for the Trident and, as the name suggests, was good enough to circumnavigate the Isle of Man at 100 mph. As per the thinking in that era, identical 4:10-19 tyres were fitted at both ends.

While that may have suited the Trident, very few of the other 1970s superbikes benefited from a set of TT100s. Less, rather than more, stability was often the result as a side effect of changing the contact patch size and shape, and altering the steering geometry to boot (as it were). Due to a distrust of Japanese tyres generally, and particularly in providing wet road grip, in Britain many owners threw away OE Dunlop Gold Seals, Inoues, Bridgestones, etc at the earliest opportunity, often before they took delivery of their new steeds. Besides being wasteful and expensive, this wasn't really a good idea. In the 1970s most large-capacity motorcycles came with a 3.25 x 19 front tyre and 4.00 x 18 rear, neither being compatible with low-profile TT100s. The later rounded profile Avon Roadrunners and Michelins were a better match.

Above: Bulletproof clutch driven directly by straight cut gear on crank, giving characteristic whistle.

Left: Once considered old people's bikes, BMW's R90S, complete with nose cone fairing, made everyone take notice.

Reflected yellow glory in a Z1 silencer. Note the removable baffles.

One of the Honda CB750's USPs in 1969 was its hydraulic front disc brake. By the time the Z1 arrived on the scene, the idea had been accepted, although the two-wheeled faction lagged behind cars, which had embraced hydraulics before the Second World War and discs in the mid-1950s. As launched in 1970, Suzuki's new GT750 still had a giant cable-operated double drum brake, but Kawasaki realised that a 550-lb, 135-mph superbike needed at least one disc.

After the initial gasp of awe, Honda's swinging caliper and stainless steel rotor had been condemned for lacking power and drastically losing efficiency in wet weather. Sadly, the Z1's front brake, a single piston floating caliper design, wasn't much better. It was possible to upgrade to twin discs as the manufacturer had thoughtfully provided attachment lugs on both fork sliders, but even that wasn't a complete solution, and it took another ten years before motorcycles had disc brakes that worked reliably when cold and wet, achieved mainly through advances in sintered friction material.

Other features of note included a large kickstart lever sprouting from the offside engine casing. The Z1 had a 210W alternator and big 14A/hr battery, but those brought up on unreliable Lucas electrics still didn't trust starter motors, so the manual option was considered essential. Even the second-generation Z1000s introduced at the end of the decade came with an emergency-use kick-start lever hidden under the seat.

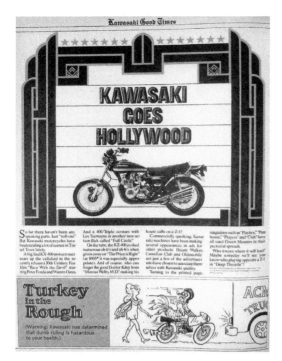

Left: US Kawasaki Good Times ad campaign, reminding us that Marcus Welby M.D. made housecalls on a Zee-One.

Below: (K)Z400 twin, Kawasaki's second four-stroke, had a completely different engine design from its four-cylinder brother.

6

The Good Times Roll

Priced at under $2,000, the Z1 arrived in US dealers in November 1972 with planned production of around 1,500 units per month The Japanese home market Z2 750 was introduced in December. Meanwhile, after debuting at the Cologne Show, the Z1 was largely unavailable in Britain for a year, just as the CB750 had been delayed, if for different reasons. Honda had the UK dealer network, but severely underestimated demand and were only able to make hundreds of Fours in 1969, not the tens of thousands required. With the luxury of two years more development time, Kawasaki was prepared for the onslaught and managed to produce about 80,000 in the first two years, including the Japan-only Z2.

Most early Z1s went to the US. UK imports were at that time handled by Agrati, a small-scale operation with a handful of dealerships that thwarted attempts to buy Kawasakis of any description. Less than fifty Z1s had been sold in Britain by 1974, when an offshoot of the parent company set up shop in Staines. Starting with only fifteen outlets, the dealer network was soon expanded and bikes became relatively easy to find. For Z1 customers the remaining obstacle was the £1,088 plus VAT price tag, around 20 per cent more than the latest CB750K2 Four. For comparison, a new Norton 850 Commando was only £727 and a Triumph Bonneville another £100 less than that.

So the Z1 was both expensive and exclusive. Was it worth a long wait and twice the price of a Bonnie? Definitely, according to *Bike* magazine in one of the few British roadtests published in the Agrati era. Indeed, part of the feature, comparing a Z1 on loan from its proud owner with a current Honda Four supplied by a dealership, was a lament about the dearth of press bikes. After airing what was no doubt justifiable criticism of the outgoing UK importer, there was no doubt in the writer's mind that the new Kawasaki was a sensation.

The only sour note was directed at the transmission, which didn't let the rider know when the gearbox was at the top or bottom of the range by having free travel in the lever, like the Honda. A small point, particularly when the CB750 had such a clunky and noisy transmission. On the same subject, but not mentioned by *Bike* in this article, Kawasaki had included an ingenious device that made it impossible to shift from first to second gear unless the bike was moving. So, no more frenzied attempts to find neutral in stop-start traffic, but there were plenty of uninformed mechanics who imagined this was a gearbox

Only the most successful high-performance big bore four-stroke engine Kawasaki ever built? Such modesty!

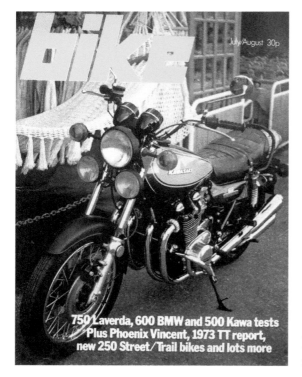

Bike managed to find a Z1 to put on the July/August 1973 cover, but the test report was still months away.

fault, not a thoughtful design feature. It's not unknown for people to strip down the entire gearbox then wonder why the same 'fault' is present when it's put back together again!

To *Bike* at least, everything else was rosy: 'Looks? This is the Gina Lollobrigida of the bike world. Handling? You'll be hanging right inside even the nimblest of 350s on any corner. Acceleration? The right-hand twist grip's connected to your own adrenal glands. Top speed? Enough to leave that siren fading into the distance.'

While the politically incorrect reference to Gina Lollobrigida proves that this was a very long time ago, it did seem that the Zed was a major step forward for motorcycling. In view of the bike's later reputation, the comments about the handling are intriguing, especially bearing in mind that this particular specimen had been fitted with TT100s. *Bike* had memorably called the H1 500 two-stroke the fastest camel in the world, and had no great hope that the bulky and heavy 900 Four would be much better, but somehow: 'The handling was perhaps the most impressive thing about the big machine, so much so that anyone who owns one might be well advised to take out the centre stand. It's just too easy to ground it.' The tester was an experienced racer, so we have to assume he knew what he was talking about.

The summary was equally complimentary: 'Kawasaki have made what looks like becoming a classic machine. It's both simple and elegant to the eye, and sophisticated in design. It is strong, a joy to ride and handles like a machine 200 lb lighter. It's incredibly fast, and, yes – safe.' Some would disagree strongly with the last point, but the first sentence shows uncanny foresight.

After a change of ownership and a revamp, *Bike* magazine compared a new (non-standard) Z1 with a Honda CB750 Four.

Celebrating a Machine of the Year award in 1974, Kawasaki Motors UK sets up shop in Staines.

Late 1973, and even the UK's biggest motorcycle dealer cant't sell you a Z1.

7

Variations on a 903cc Theme

The full set of 903 Zeds: Z1 in front, Z900 at rear, Z1A left and Z1B right.

Z1A lost the black engine cases and is arguably less attractive.

Z1A shows off its smooth belly and tucked-away exhausts.

Positively restrained behind the original.

Same badge on A, but now over Candytone Green paint.

Above: Z1B wears a new badge and Candy Super Blue livery.

Left: Z1, Z1A and Z1B used 28-mm Mikunis, Z900 dropped to 26 mm.

Honda's 750 was given a wild reception back in 1969, but familiarity soon bred contempt here in the patriotic UK. For several years all available hands had been occupied with car development, leaving the bikes out in the cold. By the time the Z1 came along, the Honda appeared to have been stuck in a timewarp and left to rest on some very withered laurels. Curiously, exactly the same fate awaited the Z1. Kawasaki did little in the way of development for four years, by which time the King was under threat from all sides, as we'll see later.

Contemporary motorcycle magazines reported that only thirty-nine of the first Z1 (frame number Z1F-000001, engine number Z1E-000001) were imported to the UK. Distinguishing features of the original include Candy Orange/Brown or Yellow/Green paintwork, and a black engine with silver alloy highlights on cylinder fins and engine cases.

The succeeding Z1A (frame number Z1F-020001, engine Z1E-020001) arrived in 1973. It had new stripy graphics, in Candytone Brown/Orange, or Candytone Green/Yellow paintwork, and an unpainted engine (probably because the black flaked off) and minor revisions to the instruments.

The Z1A, logically enough, turned into the Z1B (Frame Z1F-047500, Engine Z1E-047500) in time for Kawasaki's new UK division to shake up the dealer network and sell some serious quantities of bikes. Identifying features were another change of graphics and colour schemes. Understated Candy Super Blue or Super Red were the options. The tank badges were larger, and more subtle alterations were made to the instruments and switches. Less obviously, the rear chain oiler went in favour of a new-fangled O-ring version, which lasted for about 15,000 miles, but cost nearly £70 (at a time when fuel cost less than 70 pence a gallon) to replace and still needed lubricating on the outside. Changes to the exhausts reduced power slightly.

Unfortunately, the press horde's attitude had changed by 1974, perhaps because recent oil crises had made transport more about arriving than thrills, or fun. What use is pizzazz when there's no petrol available? When *Motorcycle Mechanics* got their oily hands on a Z1B they recorded a top speed of over 130 mph and a standing quarter in under 12.5 seconds. Yet, showing admirable restraint and responsibility, their man seemed keen to play down the performance and focus on usability instead. 'One of the three best bikes I have ever ridden,' he concluded after a 2,000 mile week, bemoaning the fact that he didn't have the necessary £1,177 to buy a Z1 himself. The only complaints concerned the tyres and lights. Again, no particular worries about the handling.

Motorcyclist Illustrated, catering for a more mature audience, was less impressed. The writer seemed disenchanted with the whole concept of superbikes and the miserable lot of motorcycle journalists, and evidently wanted to say as little as possible about the Z1, preferring to expend a few hundred words on the great British weather, which, in conjunction with Japanese tyres, made the big beast something of a liability. The suspension was 'mediocrely average', he reckoned, and the handling 'fair', but he admitted it was difficult to judge in the awful conditions experienced during the test period.

Things became more complicated in 1976 when the Z900-A4 was introduced (Frame Z1F-085701, Engine Z1E-086001). Apart from new Diamond Dark Green and Diamond Brown colour schemes, a host of changes had been made, some out of necessity as emissions and noise legislation became stricter, some as genuine improvements. For the benefit of all those who didn't rate the standard single front disc, a double-rotor set-up was standardised

What's this lever bit for, Grandpa?

Z900 had relocated battery and intake changes.

Later speedometer, calibrated in 10 mph increments.

Twin calipers was an option on Z1; UK Z900s had them as standard.

in the UK. The US KZ900 model continued with a single stopper. Note the 'KZ' prefix. At the time Kawasaki was introducing a new naming system, with model prefixes supposedly having meanings, just like Hondas. In K Speak, KE equalled Kawasaki Enduro, KX equalled Motocross, and KH equalled Highway, for instance. Somehow, the 900 escaped the new logic, apparently because it was made in Kawasaki's factory in Lincoln, Nebraska.

Whatever it was called, the Z900's new discs were 2 mm thinner than before, which gave rise to squeal and juddering as a result of wear and warpage. Other goodies included a locking fuel cap, three-way fuse system, hazard warning lights, an audible flasher indicator, square tail light and improved instruments.

The handling was generally deemed to be better, but no one really knew whether that was a result of a more rigid frame, improved suspension, different tyres, or simply that there was less power delivered with less suddenness. Officially, we did know that, by means of a quartet of 26-mm Mikunis instead of 28s, plus more restrictive exhausts and milder cam profiles, the engine had been detuned by a claimed 1 bhp. That didn't sound much, but subjectively the Z900 felt different – refined, almost, basically by having more usable midrange torque, with less of a rush when heading for the redline. The big four also seemed to have lost some of its tingling vibration (a thicker seat could have been a factor) and perhaps drank less fuel – not that that was too important, as it still went twice as far on a gallon as the previous two-stroke triples!

On the demerit side, there was no hiding the fact that ultimate performance in terms of both speed and acceleration had suffered, at least according to British road tests. Somehow, US magazine bikes just kept on going faster! Still, while the King wasn't dead yet, the throne was beginning to wobble.

Over 320 bhp of Kawasaki royalty posing in the sunshine.

Age before wisdom?

A Z900 with the author, *c.* 1979.

A much older author mounted on a Z900, 2002 (no suitable heavy lifting gear available to mirror the same pose in 2016!).

Loyal Zed subjects could console themselves that the Honda CB750 opposition was also slowing down. But elsewhere everything was speeding up. In 1976 the market was suddenly awash with rapid new European bikes. From Germany, BMW had revitalised big boxer twins. From Italy, Ducati, Moto Guzzi, Laverda and Benelli had launched a bevy of biking beauties in the form of the 900SS, Le Mans 850, Jota 1000, and 750 Sei. They were all more expensive and much more difficult to live with (despite what the Moto Guzzi ads claimed!) than Universal Japanese Motorcycles, but they had style, soul and that elusive and much-cherished quality – character.

Strange but nevertheless true, even the British had been busy and now offered a selection of characterful superbikes. BSA had effectively disappeared in 1972 but, against all the odds, Triumph's electric-start Trident T160 and Norton's Commando 850 MkIII were attractive Z900 alternatives. And don't forget the Triumph Bonneville T140, still slugging it out with the upstarts after forty years. Whisper it, but Kawasaki's four looked a bit boring in comparison.

Motorcyclist Illustrated put a Z900 through its paces and came to a confusing conclusion. After criticising the thicker seat because it made putting a foot down difficult for anyone under 6 feet tall, the vexed subject of handling arose: '...things aren't too bad, especially in the chassis department where the Z1 was so abominably unsafe at speed,' and 'Springing and damping are firmer than before and the old frightener of rear end bouncing developing into that wild, wild head wagging appears to have been killed off, at least for most conditions.' Yet after damning with faint praise, the £1,362 price tag was considered to represent amazingly good value for money (a Ducati 900SS was £1,999), and in the last paragraph the author admitted he could think of precious few changes required now.

On the road.

Two examples of engineering excellence.

Z1B, distinctive even in silhouette.

B colour schemes – not the most arresting.

8

LTD Editions and Emissions

Kawasaki had more than the renascent Europeans and British to worry about. Although Honda seemed content to update the CB750 rather than start again, much effort had obviously been poured into other capacity classes. The 1975 Gold Wing 1000, 1977 CB250/400T Dreams and CX500 V-twin showed that the R&D department hadn't been idle and were capable of innovating, even if the press were reluctant to praise. Benelli might have got there first (using a modular copy of the old SOHC Honda CB350/500 Four) but, a couple of years later, the CBX six dropped a bombshell on its Japanese rivals.

KZ750LTD, originally only for American customers but not the first 'factory custom' as claimed. The British got there first!

Kawasaki did have one trick up its corporate sleeve, however: arguably one that had far more historic importance to motorcycling. In America, the tradition was to modify and customise bikes as soon as they were bought. So why not let the manufacturer do the hard work first? Thus was born the 'factory custom', a paradox on wheels, perhaps, but one that is still with us forty years after the Kawasaki 900LTD was launched, although they tend to be called cruisers nowadays. Incidentally, fans of British bikes like to point out that the Triumph Hurricane and Norton Hi-Rider were actually the first factory customs!

Designed and built in America using quality American add-ons, the LTD was unveiled at a lush reception in Beverly Hills as the 'Street Sport Concept' and featured Morris Mag wheels, King and Queen stepped seat, a fat 5-inch rear tyre on a wide rim and trick (as they used to say) Jardine mufflers. Different side panels and a smaller tank were also essential ingredients.

Little was changed on the mechanical side, but the twin front brake calipers were mounted behind the fork sliders, the theory being that this improved stability. Most 'sport' bikes have only had sidestands for the past twenty or thirty years, but in those days it was disappointing to find that the Jardine headers went under the engine, precluding fitting a centrestand. How could you adjust the chain or take a wheel out to fix a tyre? By phoning your friendly local Kawasaki dealership and getting them to do it, was the answer.

Commando Hi-Rider
(top right) was a factory
custom...

Above: Britain led the world in factory customs! Triumph's X-75 triple just made it onto production in 1972, but the BSA X65 twin was stillborn. This is a modern replica of what might have been, built by specialist SRM in the 1990s.

Right: Norton's John Player Commando was also a sort of factory custom ...

Honda had a different interpretation. The 900 Custom had the essential fat rear tyre and baroque exhausts, but married that with Vetter touring equipment.

Despite sneers from some, Kawasaki hit the niche nail on the head here, because the 'crypto-chopper' concept was soon copied by almost every other manufacturer. Oddly enough, that included Harley. The $3,295 price tag, $800 up on the standard KZ900, didn't seem to be a deterrent. A modest initial batch of 2,000 was soon snapped up, so they made another 3,000. Not so LTD.

These were all for American consumption so the original 1976 900 (KZ900-B1 LTD, Frame: KZ900B-500011, Engine: Z1E-108503, Classic Red livery) is rare in the UK, but some later variations made it here as official imports, selling in significant numbers as a junior 440cc twin as well at the 1000cc four. The 1981 Z1000LTD shared much with the new Z1000J, including most of its reconfigured 998cc engine (now semi-rubber mounted) and strengthened chassis. Customs and what we now call cruisers had a tough time in the hands of the British press in that era. *Bike* had a KZ1000LTD on test and seemed unsure whether they should like it or not!

9

Bigger Bores

The new Z650, launched in 1976, and Z1000 were promoted together.

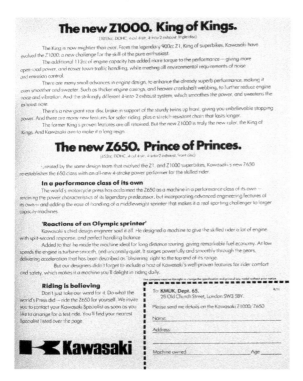

In road tests the compact 650 was found to be almost as fast as the 1000, and definitely more fun to ride.

After about a year the standard (K)Z900 was ousted by the (K)Z1000A1 (Frame: KZT00A-000001, Engine: KZT00AE-000001).

The original 903cc capacity was inconvenient at a time when UK 'rider policy' insurance became significantly more expensive for bikes over 900cc. Enlarging the bore to 68 mm gave 1015cc, which was also inconvenient for those going racing in the one-litre class.

Kawasaki's objective in expanding the engine was to preserve performance in the face of ever more stringent noise and emissions regulations. King Zed started with an endemic handicap here because roller-bearing crankshafts make more noise than plain-bearing cranks. A change in that direction was hardly practical (although Suzuki and Ducati did it, with mixed success), so other ploys had to be used.

So, the 1977 Z1000's most distinguishing feature was something it was missing, i.e. that trademark stack of four chrome silencers. Using a 4-2 system saved weight, but possibly less than expected because the two new exhausts were enormous double-skinned affairs containing lots of baffles to reduce the former bark to a more socially acceptable murmur, accompanied by the familiar primary drive whistle.

The kerb weight had risen by about 20 lb, some from extra frame strengthening around the steering head and (allegedly) thicker walled tube in places, a change that seems to have happened during the Z900's production run. Interestingly, the engine part numbers had mostly changed, even for those bits that weren't different! For example, *Cycle*'s February 1977 test reported that the cylinder head was the same, which meant there was a newly formed squish band inside the combustion chamber where it met the larger bores. Possibly this accounted for the slight rise in compression ratio, from 8.5: 1 to 8.7: 1?

Running on the same 26-mm Mikunis as the Z900, and with added crankshaft mass, the overall effect was to make the Z1000 a more civilised and relaxed machine. Nevertheless, it was *Cycle*'s fastest Kawasaki once more, clocking a standing quarter close to 12s. Again, this conflicted with the findings of the UK press. *Which Bike* recorded a top speed of 129 mph and a 12.8s quarter mile, while MCI managed only 115 mph sitting normally. It's doubtful that even the special journalistic contortions necessary to eke every last drop of performance out of test bikes would have urged more than 125 mph from that particular specimen. Perhaps it was in need of a service?

With the benefit of hindsight, MCI took time to have a scoff at other magazines' praise of the first Z1's handling. The Z1000 was much better, they reckoned, but 'no Ducati'. In the second half of the 1970s it was generally accepted that the 900SS was the ultimate in high-speed handling precision and stability, but the comparison was odorous in this case. Apart from being far more expensive, the Ducati was an uncompromising track bike with a nose-down riding position and a fairing. Even the 900SS's many fans had to admit that it only really worked properly at speeds way above the national 70 mph limit. In contrast, like nearly all Japanese bikes (the three-cylinder two-strokes being an obvious exception), the high-barred Z1000 rumbled along perfectly happily at any speed from 0 mph upwards, the upper limit being the feeling that your head was about to be ripped off your neck.

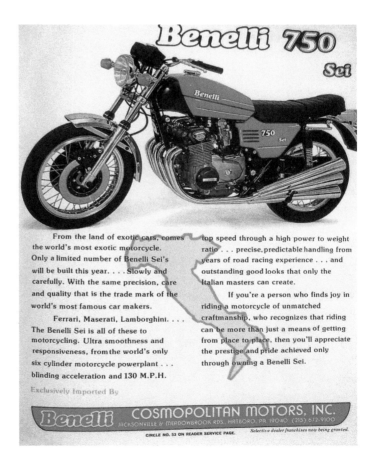

By the time the Z1000 appeared, competition was coming from all quarters, including the Benelli Sei.

Left: Enlarged 900 version of the Italian six – also a threat.

Below: Ducati's 900SS and Hailwood Replica offered a completely different type of motorcycling.

Above: The Laverda Jota 1000, specially developed for the British market, clocked 140 mph and could be heard in the next county.

Right: The superbike shopping list had to include Moto Guzzi's sublime Le Mans 850.

10

Z1-R: A New Angle

Aside from Italian bikes, the main threat for Kawasaki by this stage was the arrival of direct competition from other Japanese manufacturers, all with DOHC, all as fast or faster. Yamaha had the shaft drive XS750 triples and XS1100 fours, Honda had the CBX six, and Suzuki's GS750 and GS1000 fours offered tempting alternatives. The GS1000 comprehensively bettered the standard Z1000 in every department. It was a little unfair that Suzuki seemed to have used a rebadged Kawasaki engine, but that's business!

'Swoopy' Z1000 was joined by the chiselled Z1-R in 1978, not to everyone's approval.

Avon Roadrunners.
Superboots for Superbikes.

Roadrunners are the new breed of tyre, as power and performance oriented as the true superbikes.

H – rated, 130 mph tyres, made from Avon's exclusive high hysteresis 'cling rubber' to give you confidence to lay your super-bike over.

Championship-winning tyres with chunky reinforced shoulder blocks and a classically bold tread pattern so that you can burn up the road without burning up your tyres.

And that's no idle boast. Many riders have found that Roadrunners deliver up to 50% more mileage than the best competitive tyres.

For the sake of your bike, and your pocket, check out Roadrunners now.

16"	17"	18"	19"
5.10 H 16	3.10 H 17	3.10 H 18	3.60 H 19
	*5.10 H 17	3.60 H 18	4.10 H 19
	Available shortly	4.10 H 18	
		4.25/85 H 18	
		4.70 H 18	

BIKE ON AVON

New Avon Roadrunners were suitable for the Z1-R and a diverse range of others, but were not always the perfect match.

Fighting back, the Z1-R was released in 1978 as a take on the European café racer image, as conceived back in 1974. (Z1000-D1 Z1R, Frame: KZT00D-000001, Engine: KZT00DE-000001). Only one colour was available: Metallic Stardust Silver, rather like the BMW R100RS. Most of the changes were cosmetic: 18-inch alloy wheels at both ends, angular tank and cockpit fairing, new instruments, and a 4-1 exhaust terminating in a vast silencer. The engine was back to black like the first Z1 (except with a more durable finish that didn't flake off first time it rained) and had reverted to 28-mm carbs, taking maximum power to 90 bhp at 8,000 rpm.

The styling wasn't everyone's cup of coffee, and the £2,000 price tag, £200 more than the plain Z1000, was a hindrance, especially when coupled with some less than euphoric test reports. *Motor Cycle Mechanics* apparently had their test victim in the middle of a freezing winter, exposing the deficiencies of the fairing to fend off the cold or the new drilled discs to work when soaked in icy water. The handling wasn't particularly good either, and a small 2.9 g petrol tank drastically limited the range, even though the engine was quite frugal as well as powerful. In response to customer feedback, a larger tank holding just over 4 g was made available, but that failed to boost sales, so some Z1-Rs lingered in shops for several years, by which time the rest of the world had moved on again. 'I'm afraid it looks as if the King is dying,' was the unflattering verdict.

The Z's.
There is no substitute.

No substitute for the visual turn-on of the Z-1000 LTD. It hits you where you live. Powerful and demanding of respect. The LTD. Try to catch one.

No substitute for the experience of riding the Z-1000. It's everything you've dreamed about in motorcycling. Power. Handling. Reliability. The Z-1000. To ride one is catching.

No substitute for the Z1-R. Period. One look and your mouth forms a natural "wow". Get the rest of the wows at your dealer's. The Z1-R. Now they'll never catch up.

Kawasaki
We know why you ride.

MODEL SUBJECT TO LIMITED AVAILABILITY.   KAWASAKI BELIEVES IN RIDING SAFELY. CHECK LOCAL LAWS BEFORE YOU RIDE.

Z1R IS HERE

Z1R. New from Kawasaki. The way it looks is beautiful. And so is the way it goes.

Z1R is for the few riders who can handle the increased power pumped out by the awesome 1015cc engine—developed from the unburstable DOHC four of the legendary Z1000.

Power that pushes the Z1R to acceleration times and a top speed that break new frontiers even for us.

Z1R is for the rider who appreciates totally functional styling, from the razor edge quarter fairing with its smoked windscreen and integrated instruments, through the clean, slim lines of the tank to the smooth upswept tail. All in custom quicksilver blue. And from the machined cast alloy wheels with drilled discs front and rear to the mean matt black finish on that mighty cylinder block with the four into two into one exhaust.

Z1R is built for sheer performance, for sheer handling and for sheer style. And Z1R means that at last you can judge a bike's performance by the way it looks—sensational.

Kawasaki
Let the good times roll

Above: The comprehensive US Kawasaki 1000 range.

Left: Americans tended to call it Z1R, not Z1-R.

Meanwhile, our man on the Bonneville Salt Flats was still relishing the prospect of kick-starting his engine. Don't laugh, because the T140 was the top-selling 750 in the UK.

The Triumph Trident T160 and Mk3 Norton Commando had sadly disappeared by 1978.

Bike's test was more positive, although again the drilled discs and high-tech brake pads were found to be no improvement. The revitalised engine was probably the best feature, powering the 560 lb beast to 132 mph on the long Snetterton straight, and clocking the fastest standing quarter in the magazine's seven-year history. An even faster sub-12s run would have been attainable in better conditions, they reckoned, but did potential customers really care about figures that had little relevance to everyday motorcycling? No, judging by sales.

11

Diversification

After seven years of essentially minor updates, in 1979 Kawasaki finally gave the King a complete makeover. The first major update was the MkII, launched in tandem with the 1000ST shaft-drive tourer. Apart from the basic front half of the engine (although note that the distinctive round cam housings at the side of the cylinder head were now more rectangular), the two differed in almost every respect and shared few components. Frame, wheels, bodywork, suspension, brakes, instruments, exhausts and cosmetics: all new, all different.

Changing from chain to shaft drive obviously involved major alterations to the engine, which in turn meant the frame and swinging arm also had to be new, but Kawasaki gave

Beaten to the shops by the Benelli Sei and Honda CBX, in 1979 the gargantuan Z1300 had the same sort of role as the new shaft drive Z1000ST.

By the time the 1000ST arrived, Honda's Gold Wing was already established as the touring riders' favourite.

the ST uprated suspension in line with its new touring role. In practice, the chain-drive MkII was often considered superior to the ST for long-distance comfort and stability, while the shaft drive version was faster! In pre-O-ring days, having to adjust a chain every few hundred miles would have been a handicap, but that wasn't a factor now.

To be blunt, neither the MkII (Z1000-A3, Frame, KZT00A-038427, Engine KZT00AE-081566) nor ST (Z1000-E1, Frame KT00E-000101, Engine KZT00EE-000101) sold very well. There was too much competition and the market was shrinking. Having peaked in 1979, UK motorcycle sales were now heading for a long period of decline. Changes in legislation aimed at reducing accidents forced learner riders onto restricted 125s, so the 250cc L-plate class collapsed. Allowing completely clueless seventeen year olds to ride 90 mph bikes with no training was obviously a bad idea now that the roads were so busy, but addressing that issue upset the whole market order. 250s were a natural stepping stone to 500s and 750s, but a learner on a 125 was more likely to move to a 350 or 400 – or, as became apparent, give up bikes and buy a warm, dry car instead. As a result, the average age of motorcyclists crept up, a process that has continued ever since. Instead of being a teenagers' pastime, the core buyers in the 1980s, 1990s, 2000s and 2010s are the very same people who roamed the roads forty years ago on mopeds as teenagers, L-plates flapping.

Aside from the upheavals in the motorcycle market generally, it has to be said that the MkII and ST were perceived as being dull. 93 bhp in 1979 was a lot less impressive than 82 bhp in 1972. The various colour options, Luminous Navy Blue, Luminous Dark Red and Luminous Green, coupled with restrained graphics, were a world away from the bold original. Fashions may change, but goths didn't rush out to buy big Kawasakis, it seems.

66

1000ST and its chain-drive brother were surprisingly different, but neither sold very well.

ST had calipers behind new leading-axle forks.

Heavy shaft transmission didn't help the handling.

Rear disc instead of drum, but it still didn't work in the rain.

After another increase in bore to 72.5 mm, the 1000ST transmogrified into the 1089cc Z1100A1 (Frame KZT10A-000001, Engine KZT10AE-000001, available in Luminous Navy or Luminous Passion Red). In some respects this was similar to the LTD series, although touring was the goal. That didn't stop the rechristened *Mechanics* magazine from submitting a Z1100A to one of its flat-out 24-hour tests, up against a bevy of bikes more suited to racetracks. All things considered, it acquitted itself well, blowing off the opposition on the straight then losing it all by tying itself in knots in corners. Reliability seemed fine, though, as expected of any descendant of the Z1. That belief, however, was about to be blown apart!

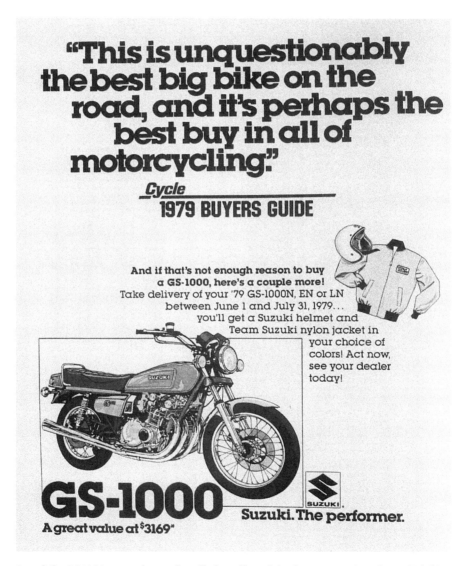

Suzuki's GS1000 was cheap, handled well and had a reputation for reliability, perhaps because its engine was very like a Z1's.

OCTOBER 1979 60p USA $2.75

Giant Test: Six
bike 16er Shootout

**Highlands,
Islands And Thousands**
24 Hours Round A Spanish Park

Bike heads off to Scotland on the new Z1000ST and MkII with a Vetter touring kit.

12

Abdication

In 1980 the MkII and ST were joined by the Z1000H, which was similar to the MkII except that it was fitted with fuel injection instead of Mikuni carburettors. A world first for motorcycles (beating Honda's CX500 Turbo to market by a year), but you did have to wonder why anyone would pay about 15 per cent more for something that gave no better performance and would be difficult to fix if it went wrong.

The full model designation included an EFI suffix, meaning Electronic Fuel Injection, in this case a Japanese version of the Bosch K-Jetronic system already familiar on cars. While it might have seemed like a technological dream at the time, thirty-six years later it looks very quaint, particularly the large control module festooned with discrete components hidden under the rear seat. Despite the name, EFI relied on mechanical fuel metering and air flow sensing. Unlike later systems that monitor all aspects of an engine, there was no interaction with the ignition.

Fitting fuel injection to a car like the VW Golf GTi gave about 20 per cent more power and made the engine generally more responsive. Fitting it to the Kawasaki Z1000H (or US Z1000G, a model half way between the standard and LTD) made virtually no difference to the performance while it dulled the response. Bikes were as yet subject to far less strict emissions standards, so, apart from the initial appeal to customers who always had to have the latest, it seemed Kawasaki was looking to the future, when all engines would have to have fuel injection. A more cynical view was that customers were just being used as unofficial R&D engineers.

Kawasaki sold 15,000 bikes in 1979, but the motorcycling outlook was less than rosy. Registrations were in decline across the board, and Big K's various superbikes needed a fresh USP. Things changed completely in 1981 thanks to the GPz range, spearheaded by the 108 bhp GPz1100B1. Like the Z1100A, capacity was up to 1089cc from a 72.5-mm bore. That was just the start of it, because the frame tubes and fork stanchions were stronger, the valves were bigger, the cam chain was a hy-vo, the gearbox had been beefed up, the crankshaft was lighter, the instruments were new, the suspension was air-assisted, etc, etc. Almost a new motorcycle.

Motorcycle Mechanics recorded a standing quarter in comfortably under 12s, with a top speed of 144 mph, so there was no doubt the injected engine gave more power. The slimmed

In motorcycles, as with anything else, you get exactly what you pay for.

That's why the three year old Harley-Davidson FX sold for $100 more than its original sticker price.

And why it sold for $300 more than the 1975 Z-1, Kawasaki's best.

As a matter of fact, the original Kawasaki owner traded up to a Harley-Davidson after less than 350 miles on his Z-1.

He wasn't happy with second best. Few people are.

What keeps Harley-Davidson on top? Some say styling. Others, engineering. Still others talk about pure value; the rider gets more of what he pays for.

The plain fact is that people are willing to pay a premium price for the best. And they show sound judgement by riding the finest.

When they're ready to trade-in, they know their Harley-Davidson is worth top dollar. It retains its value like no other bike we know of.

Discover the Harley-Davidson difference. Visit your AMF Harley-Davidson dealer. He's got the bikes. The 125cc's through the legendary 1200cc superbikes.

You'll be buying value. And, in motorcycles, that means Harley-Davidson. Period.

Harley-Davidson

The Great American Freedom Machines.

Harley-Davidson believes in safety first. Before you start out, light your lights, put on your helmet and watch out for the other guy.

CIRCLE NO. 25 ON READER SERVICE PAGE.

After a long decline, Harley began to claw back customers in the 1980s.

down chassis was generally liked, but the modified gearbox failed to impress. In summary: 'Kawasaki are certainly getting things right with their handling and general ride comfort. In this respect, I think the GPz1100 represents both the end of the big-motor development and the beginning of a new line of machines which will concentrate on chassis design and general usability.' With the benefit of another helping of 20/20 hindsight, that seems fair enough.

Besides performance, it was the instantly recognisable red colour schemes that made the GPz range such a success. While Suzuki's new GSX1100 probably did everything at least as well as the Kawasaki and had sixteen valves tucked away in its cylinder head, it looked staid. The GPz1100 was the big seller, but also new was the Z1000J, billed as an affordable, no-frills sports bike (with 34-mm carbs, not EFI), priced at £2,349. That was only about £200 less than its red showroom mate, and it had fewer of the latest goodies, so what was the point? 69.44-mm cylinder bores was the answer, reducing the capacity from 1015cc to 998cc as required for some racing formulae; F1, for instance.

1982's GPz1100B2 wasn't very different, except for the appearance of a small cockpit fairing, guaranteed to worsen the high-speed weave noted on the B1. The fuel injection, however, was a completely revised system, using a barrage of sensors and digital mapping instead of a mechanical air flow meter and a pump. An altogether more sophisticated set-up, yet only worth 1 bhp!

Suzuki GS1000 turned into GSX1100 in 1980 – direct competition for the GPz1100.

No sooner had the ink on the cheques in Kawasaki dealers dried on the B2 than the third and final GPz1100 arrived, complete with Uni-Trak rear suspension. Not to be outdone, the engine had been completely reworked yet again. For the first time, the tappet shims were positioned under the buckets, as on the smaller fours. This removed fears of shims popping out at high revs, which would have been more likely now because the cams were bumpier and the compression ratio higher, giving 120 bhp at 8,750 rpm – some 50 per cent above the first Z1.

The demonic engine went into a new frame, modified to accept a monoshock rear end, which now used a box-section aluminium swinging arm. Leading the way, the forks had anti-dive. The latter was a largely useless aberration of the early 1980s, along with 16-inch wheels, but most of the rest was worthwhile. The GPz was a long and large machine, the spindle span now being nearly 62 inches; yet, topped off by a bigger fairing and a curved styling theme to the graphics, the result was a bike that had more rear-wheel horsepower than anything else available, did almost 150 mph flat out and could clock standing quarters in less than 11 seconds. Or at least, that's what they managed in the US. Once again, the Brits were slower. *Bike* managed 10 mph less and failed to make the Uni-Trak go as fast on the dragstrip as the previous B2.

Ducati V-twins faded away in the 1980s.

Figures apart, the final GPz1100 incarnation had a different personality. The engine had to be revved past 6,000 rpm before it gave much power, so it was slower in most circumstances unless you were prepared to change gear a lot. Which made it a shame that the transmission was worse. Still, it was almost certainly the best handling, most stable of the bunch – provided the air suspension was set up properly, which wasn't easy.

The GPz had a close cousin, generally referred to as the Eddie Lawson Replica. Based on the KZ1000J with added GPz1100 ingredients, the KZ1000R celebrated Mr L's 1982 factory-backed victory in the AMA Superbike class. If that wasn't enough, a select few could buy something closer to the actual bike raced, the KZ1000S1, with about 140 bhp on tap.

The first 1982 models were for the USA only, but in 1983 the rest of the world could buy one, although as Eddie had now signed for Yamaha, it was, rather confusingly, more likely to be white than the lime green factory colours. *Bike*'s test included a memorable series of photos showing how to fall off a Z1000R2 by running out of ground clearance, but that wasn't obligatory. Disappointingly, they only managed a top speed of 126 mph and 12.3s standing quarter, slightly down on the figures achieved by the original Z1 ten years earlier.

While Kawasaki continued to supply bikes to police forces, as made famous by the *CHiPs* TV series, 1984 was the end of the superbike (or sumobike) era. Honda had brought out V4s

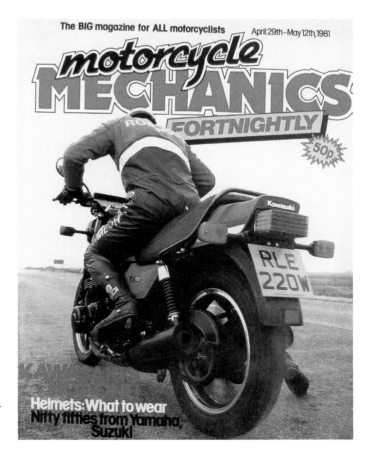

Motorcycle Mechanics temporarily goes fortnightly and tests the new GPz1100 B1.

that made high-speed motorcycling so much easier. Then Kawasaki made the big GPz1100 look like a lumbering antique by launching the GPz750 Turbo and water-cooled GPZ900R.

Showing that the Z1 was a fond memory for so many, in 1991 Kawasaki launched the Zephyr range of 'retros'. Available in 550, 750 and 1100 capacities, these were designed to look like the sort of muscle machine that bikers rode in the late 1970s and 1980s – in other words, modified Zeds with aftermarket alloy wheels, remote reservoir rear shocks, box-section swinging arms and four-into-something exhausts. Later versions aped the original Z1 look, with back-to-1973 candy colours and graphics, plus wire wheels. Despite appearances, the engines owed more to the plain bearing crank Z650 and had a different character to rumbly old King Zed.

As another tribute to the past, in the last year of the millennium Kawasaki gave us the ZRX1100, a sort of updated version of the 1982 Eddie Lawson Replica. Based on the 1052cc ZZ-R1100 water-cooled engine, this model didn't have a direct link with the past, but it sold well and even started a few racing careers. A capacity increase to 1164cc was inevitable, and later models came in two guises. The ZRX1200S version had a half fairing, while the ZRX1200R came with a bikini-nose cone inspired by the original Eddie machine – and to wallow in nostalgia completely you could have one painted lime green, naturally!

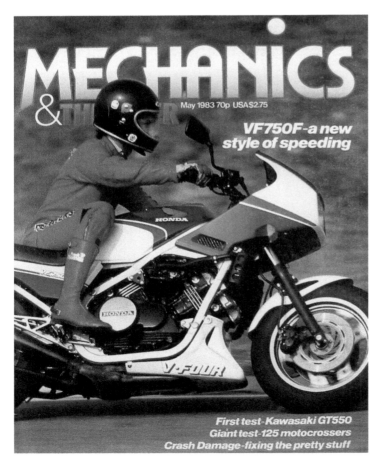

All change in 1983. Honda's VF750F was great when it was going, but its natural habitat turned out to be a Five Star workshop.

13

Improving the Breed

The Z1 immediately attracted the attention of racers and tuners. Honda's Four had already been persuaded to produce far more power, but the Kawasaki obviously had more potential thanks to its extra capacity, bulletproof roller-bearing crankshaft, shorter stroke and double camshafts. 100 bhp and more was easily possible. On the face of it, if you wanted to go faster there was little reason to make life difficult and stay with Honda, apart from brand loyalty.

Russ Collins turbo kits.

Daytona Speed week, early in 1973, was where it all began, with Kawasaki fielding the cream of its factory riders. A team comprising Cliff Carr, Gary Nixon, Art Baumann, Hurley Wilvert and Cook Neilson (editor of *Cycle*, and an accomplished racer) took the 24-hour record, clocking an average speed of 109.641 mph. Two bikes were run, both standard apart from Koni rear dampers and lower handlebars. In the hands of Yvon du Hamel, another Z1 mildly breathed upon by the legendary Pops Yoshimura lapped at over 160 mph, reaching 175 mph on the banking.

Although there was little chance of buying a Z1 in Britain, this feat was enough to convince the readership of *MotorCycle News* to vote it Machine of the Year, finally displacing the Norton Commando after five wins. Kawasaki 900s and 1000s took the title for four years.

King Zed inevitably became the weapon of choice in the growing craze for endurance racing in Europe. 1974 was the peak of its career, with first, third and fifth in the Le Mans 1,000 km. A couple of months later an Egli framed Z1 was victorious at the Barcelona 24 Horas. The September finale was a fight between BMW and Kawasaki. Out of sixty starters, eighteen were Z1 powered, including the entry from long-distance maestros Godier and Genoud, a bored-out one-litre motor in an Egli chassis. Some of the privateers were running with near 1200cc, but that tipped the balance too far towards fragility. Du Hamel's Kaw had a series of problems and was running well behind. The two works BMWs suffered the same way, one breaking its transmission, the other having a crankshaft disaster. Godier and Genoud found the right compromise once again and finished first.

The standard floating single-piston caliper front brake was less powerful than ideal to arrest a 550 lb plus rider travelling at 130mph. Optional twin discs better.

The wins continued. In 1975, Dave Aldana and his famous skeleton leathers (much criticised for bad taste) took the Daytona proddie event. The Z1's enlargement to 1015cc for the Z1000 promised more success, starting with a victory in the Australian 6-hour production race. Also in the other half of the globe, a young Graeme Crosby was creating waves by riding his bog-standard Z1000 to the circuit, going flat out for six hours and winning!

Godier and Genoud continued with their Kawasaki allegiance and experimented with radical chassis, but ultimately were overcome by the might (and budget) of Honda's RCBs. The tables were turned in the early 1980s, when Jean-Claude Chemarin deserted Honda for Kawasaki.

Meanwhile, in America, Reg Pridmore and his Z1000 became hard to beat in the late 1970s and, with factory backing, 'Steady' Eddie Lawson twice won the AMA Superbike Championship, in 1982 inspiring Kawasaki to produce a replica of the winning bike, basically a heavily modified Z1000J (KZ1000J in the US, as described elsewhere).

Drag racers of the same era also appreciated the DOHC engine, most notably the Dutch Kawasaki importer Henk Vink, who in 1981 became the first in Europe to crack the 7-second standing quarter barrier.

Taking a different route, in 1975 a small California-based company called American Turbo-Pak offered bolt-on turbocharger kits for the Z1. For around $1,000 you got a RayJay turbo and Bendix carb, plus all the extra plumbing, terminating in an open exhaust (the 'fan' in the headers has a silencing effect, luckily). To prevent meltdown, the compression

Motor Cycle Mechanics tests a tuned Rickman Z1 and comes away disappointed.

ratio was reduced to 7.5:1. Exactly how much power produced was dependent on the maximum boost pressure, but over 100 bhp was delivered to the rear wheel with 10 psi.

Renowned American drag racer and showman Russ Collins also produced a bolt-on turbo kit for the big fours, costing nearly $1,500 but good for a 9.33s, 153 mph standing quarter. Despite the performance, the conversion, also available for the Z1000 and Suzuki GS1000, was said to be completely happy on the road.

Perhaps, but in Britain we preferred to concentrate on more traditional tuning techniques. Celebrated go-faster experts Paul Dunstall and the Rickman brothers were quickly on the Z1 case. In 1975 *Motorcycle Mechanics* tested the full house S&S tuned Rickman, complete with fibreglass bodywork and £2,103 price tag. Bored to 1073cc, fitted with bumpier cams, 10:1 pistons and electronic ignition, around 100 bhp was on the cards, together with a top speed of 140-plus mph and a standing quarter mile of less than 12 seconds. On the day, however, the performance fell short of expectations. While the 12s dead quarter recorded was good, the big beast only managed to struggle to 125 mph, despite a fairing that in theory would reduce drag. Further development needed there.

In the early 1980s, at about the time the Z1 was fading into the background, tuners were still learning new tricks. Tony Huck, press officer of the British Drag Racing Association, developed his Z900 into a 1198cc beast with 13.5:1 compression ratio and camshafts like the Alps. Revving to over 10,000 rpm and producing around 150 bhp, much of the rest of the engine was standard, apart from precautionary welded crankpins. Even the clutch could cope with 8,000 rpm launches and a terminal standing quarter speed of over 140 mph! Now that's tough.

In the 1970s, Z1 based bikes ruled endurance racing until Honda muscled in.

Z1000R, hit Britain in 1983, but initially only in white, not Eddie Lawson lime green.

street bikes '84

SPORTS RANGE

Z1100R

Model: Z1100-R1. **Engine:** Four cylinder four stroke of 1089cc capacity. DOHC. Transistorised ignition with electronic advance. Max power 114hp @ 8,500rpm. Five speed gearbox. **Suspension:** Front: Single inflation point, air adjustable tele-forks, 145mm travel. Rear: Twin shock absorbers with remote reservoirs. 100mm wheel travel. **Wheels:** Front: 18in. Rear: 18in. Tubeless tyres. **Brakes:** Front: Twin discs, 246mm dia. Rear: 236mm dia. **Dimensions:** Wheelbase 1540mm, seat height 785mm, dry weight 238kg, fuel capacity 21.4 litres. **Colours:** Lime Green or Stardust Silver.

Z1000J

Model: Z1000-J3. **Engine:** Four cylinder four stroke of 998cc capacity. DOHC. Transistorised ignition. Max power 102hp @ 8,500rpm. Five speed gearbox. **Suspension:** Front: Single inflation point, air adjustable tele-forks, 145mm travel. Rear: Twin shock absorbers, 100mm wheel travel. **Wheels:** Front: 19in. Rear: 18in. Tubeless tyres. **Brakes:** Front: Twin discs, 243mm dia. Rear: 236mm dia disc. **Dimensions:** Wheelbase 1520mm, seat height 805mm, dry weight 233kg, fuel capacity 21.4 litres. **Colours:** Candy Cobalt Blue or Metallic Starlight Black.

Z650

Model: Z650-F4. **Engine:** Four cylinder four stroke of 652cc capacity. DOHC. Transistorised ignition. Max power 67hp @ 9,000rpm. Five speed gearbox. **Suspension:** Front: Air adjustable tele-forks, 160mm travel. Rear: Twin shock absorbers, 95mm wheel travel. **Wheels:** Front: 19in. Rear: 18in. Tubeless tyres. **Brakes:** Front: Twin discs, 226mm dia. Rear: 180mm dia drum. **Dimensions:** Wheelbase 1440mm, seat height 820mm, dry weight 209kg, fuel capacity 16.5 litres. **Colours:** Candy Wine Red or Galaxy Silver.

SPORTS RANGE

Z1000R

Model: Z1000-R2. **Engine:** Four cylinder four stroke of 998cc capacity. DOHC. Transistorised ignition. Max power 104hp @ 8,500rpm. Five speed gearbox. **Suspension:** Front: Single inflation point, air adjustable tele-forks, 145mm travel. Rear: Twin shock absorbers with remote reservoirs, 100mm wheel travel. **Wheels:** Front: 19in. Rear: 18in. Tubeless tyres. **Brakes:** Front: Twin discs, 246mm dia. Rear: 236mm dia disc. **Dimensions:** Wheelbase 1520mm, seat height 785mm, dry weight 236kg, fuel capacity 21.4 litres. **Colour:** Polar White.

Z750

Model: Z750-L4. **Engine:** Four cylinder four stroke of 738cc capacity. DOHC. Transistorised ignition. Max power 80hp @ 9,500rpm. Five speed gearbox. **Suspension:** Front: Air adjustable tele-forks, 150mm travel. Rear: Twin shock absorbers, 111mm wheel travel. **Wheels:** Front: 19in. Rear: 18in. Tubeless tyres. **Brakes:** Front: Twin discs, 226mm dia. Rear: 226mm dia disc. **Dimensions:** Wheelbase 1460mm, seat height 800mm, dry weight 215kg, fuel capacity 21.7 litres. **Colour:** Ebony.

Z550F

Model: ZR550-A2. **Engine:** Four cylinder four stroke of 553cc capacity DOHC. Transistorised ignition. Max power 56hp @ 9,000rpm. Six speed gearbox. **Suspension:** Front: Single inflation point, air adjustable tele-forks, 175mm travel. Rear: Uni-Trak, 140mm wheel travel. **Wheels:** Front: 19in. Rear: 18in. Tubeless tyres. **Brakes:** Front: Twin discs 242mm dia. Rear: 160mm dia drum. **Dimensions:** Wheelbase 1450mm, seat height 795mm, dry weight 184kg, fuel capacity 18.5 litres. **Colours:** Ebony or Candy Cardinal Red.

◼◀Kawasaki

1984 range included both Z1000R2 and Z1100R1.

82

14

King Not Dead

After many years of being largely ignored, Japanese bikes finally became accepted as 'classic' and part of the show scene.

Even when motorcycle registrations were declining from their 1979 peak, the Z1 never completely lost its allure, as happened to the Honda CB500 and 750 fours. Partly that was due to the bombproof reputation of its engine. In a worst-case scenario, the big DOHC motor could be rescued and transplanted into something else, modified to suit. Originally listed at around £1,200 in the UK, early Z1s held much of their value in figures, if not in reality, after factoring in the crippling inflation suffered in the 1970s, when the pound in your pocket was worth significantly less every day.

A 1978 'buyers' guide' in down-to-earth *Motorcycle Mechanics* boldly predicted that a 1973 Z1 'may have some small rarity value eventually'. About forty years later, the writer would be amused to see some early Zeds selling for over £20,000! That sounds and is impressive, but remember that the 1978 going rate of £900 is the equivalent of about £5,000 now. Nevertheless, it's plain that during the last couple of decades a Z1 or Z900 has been one of the best and safest places to salt away money.

Yet it would be a shame to think of bikes merely as part of an investment portfolio. Kawasaki created the Z1 to let the good times roll, so it's disappointing that so many are becoming motionless motorcycles. There's no excuse, because although some iconic relics from the more distant past are very tricky to ride on cluttered modern roads, Z1s, Z900s and their offshoots make eminently practical everyday transport. Indeed, many recent and current models are far less usable, a trend that began shortly after the GPz1100 Uni-Trak was terminated.

We can blame Suzuki's GSX-R750 for the 'race replica' concept. All the rest jumped on the bandwagon, and for some reason British bikers in particular decided that what they really needed was a machine that could lap the TT course at 120 mph, but was purgatory

In 1984 old King Zed was replaced by new King Zed. Water-cooled GPZ900Rs offered 150 mph top speed and fine handling, making the outgoing GPz1100 Uni-Trak look like a dinosaur.

to ride in traffic. As a consequence, many of these 'plastic rockets' had the use pattern of a lawnmower and covered a similar number of miles per year.

As previously mentioned, good early Zeds sell for over £20,000 – well over for mint condition specimens. Even a complete bike in need of restoration might have a five-figure price tag. Such is the demand and parts supply situation that specialists can rebuild a concourse bike from scratch. After hundreds of painstaking person/hours, the finished article will actually be better than new, as Kawasaki paint and chrome was strictly rationed in the 1970s. Superior results can be achieved today.

Original exhausts usually fell apart or rusted away internally before chrome blemishes appeared, but replacements are available. The current price is around £1,300, but a set of King Zed bugles has such a major effect on a bike's value that it can be a wise investment.

Much of the 'what goes wrong' type of buying advice given by motorcycle magazines in the 1970s and '80s is irrelevant now. For instance, things like leaky fork seals, worn chains and duff electrics are mere trifles. Unless you're buying a relatively cheap restoration project or 'barn find' (the barns tend to be in America, of course, but the main Z1 traffic goes back towards Japan nowadays), start by making a careful check on the bike's identity. Most importantly, do the frame and engine/crankcases belong to each other and the rest of the assemblage? Apparently small departures from original spec can make a big difference. Most parts are available, but, as a legacy from the days when

Unlike the Honda CB750, the Z's top end can be removed with the engine in the frame.

bikes were customised by throwing away exhausts and intake plumbing, some OE spares are like gold dust.

Mechanically, the big four built a reputation for invincibility during the 1970s, but it isn't the most silent of engines, thanks to all the roller bearings. In those days probably the worst that could happen was a twisted crankshaft, an unlikely event unless the engine was heavily tuned, in which case the solution was welded crankpins. In contrast to contemporary Hondas, the cam chain rarely gave trouble. If the top end went wrong, it was usually the result of a botched DIY attempt to adjust the valve clearances.

However, an engine that still has ancient cam chain guides and jockey wheels lurking inside is a liability. No matter how few miles it's covered, old age will make the plastic parts crack and break up. If in doubt, replace. Which might be when you discover the Achilles heel of old Japanese bikes: stuck cylinder barrels and engine bolts! The problem is that the holding down studs corrode and refuse to part company with the barrels. If only they could have let engines ooze protective oil like British bikes. Funnily enough, early Z1s did often leak from the head joint, but they cured it with a modified gasket. Spoilsports.

Alternators, regulators/rectifiers and wiring harnesses aren't entirely blameless, but the Z1 has a simple electrical system, so faults here are relatively easily fixed. Rebuildable spoked wheels are another godsend in the classic era. The alloy wheels that came later in the 1970s are heavy and prone to damage. According to lore, early frames sometimes cracked near the headstock, possibly as a result of fitting engine protection bars and falling off. Others claim it happened spontaneously due to vibration, but the problem does seem to have been exaggerated.

Unfortunately, the Z1 picture of reliability fell apart in more ways than one after 1981, when the Z1000J and GPz1100 arrived, complete with an extensive catalogue of woes. Firstly, the paintwork was poor, both on the tank and elsewhere. As part of the new image, the exhausts were sprayed heat-resistant matt black, but after a few days it looked dreadful. Something more lasting than supplying dealers with pots of paint was required, pronto, so the next GPz had shiny black chrome exhausts. Much better, except that the baffles disintegrated.

As did alternators and rotors, which could damage the crank. Dropping out of gear was also a favourite party trick that could result in bent valves and/or a twisted crank. Then there was heavy oil consumption, apparently caused by distorted cylinder liners. A pint of oil disappearing in a few hundred miles was typical, and unacceptable for a new £2,500 bike.

There were plenty of other issues, all seemingly rooted in a move to cut costs and rush new models into production. Kawasaki wasn't the only company suffering such an embarrassment, though. Hondas of this vintage were also dreadfully unreliable. The first 750 V4s and CBX550 were warranty claims on wheels, and Yamaha had its share of disasters, leading to some models quickly disappearing without trace.

Happily, by the end of the decade, all the Japanese Big Four had sorted out their problems. Kawasaki probably led the way here because the GPz1100's replacement, the GPZ900R 'Ninja' available from 1984, followed the original Z1's example and has since established itself as a worthy successor.

Long live the next King.

GO BACK TO THE FUTURE.

The new Kawasaki Zephyr 750 and 550s recapture the kind of raw motorcycling we built our reputation on in the '70s. But now, that heritage is more refined, more practical and more usable. It's back to the open road, the wind in your open-face, deep chrome and a paint job so rich, it reflects what classic biking's all about. At the heart beats the proven simplicity of air-cooled DOHC in-line fours, tuned for mid-range power, sitting in double cradle, high tensile steel frames. You get electric starting and legendary Kawasaki stopping. A big fat seat and a natural riding position. After all, who needs a hell for leather bike when you can have heaven in leather on a Zephyr? Supply will be limited, so visit your local Authorised Kawasaki Dealer soon, or call CXCO 500245 for a free brochure on all 31 Kawasakis. With the Zephyrs you'll find nostalgia isn't what it used to be.

Kawasaki

In 1992 Kawasaki launched the Zephyr range as a tribute to the Z1.

Specification (1973 Z1)

Engine:
Air-cooled, four-cylinder, double overhead camshaft
Bore and stoke: 66 mm x 66 mm
Capacity: 903cc
Compression ratio: 8.5:1
Power: 82 bhp at 8,500 rpm
Torque: 54lb/ft at 7,000 rpm
Carburettors: four Mikuni 28 mm

Transmission:
Gearbox: five-speed constant mesh
Ratios:
1st 12.79:1
2nd 8.84:1
3rd 6.74:1
4th 5.58:1
5th 4.92:1
Primary drive: Gear

Chassis:
Welded steel twin cradle
Front suspension: 36 mm oil damped fork
Rear suspension: oil damped coil springs, five-way

Brakes:
Front 296 disc, floating caliper
Rear single leading shoe 200 mm drum

Dimensions:
Length: 2,207 mm
Width: 813 mm
Wheelbase: 1,499 mm
Seat height: 800 mm
Kerb weight: 249 kg

Wheels:
Spoked wire, chrome-plated steel rims

Tyres:
Front 3.25 x 19 in
Rear 4.00 x 18 in

Electrical

12v negative earth

Ignition: twin contact breakers firing two cylinders using wasted spark system

Charging: 210W alternator

Battery: 14A/hr

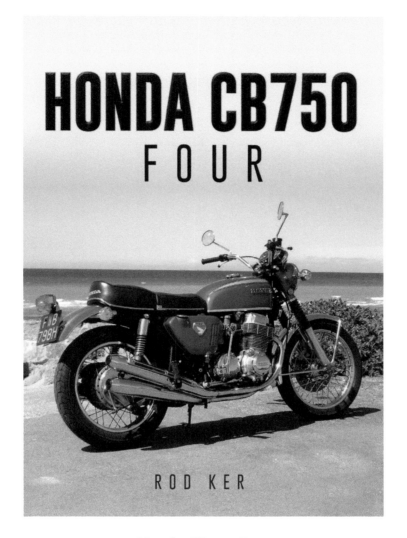

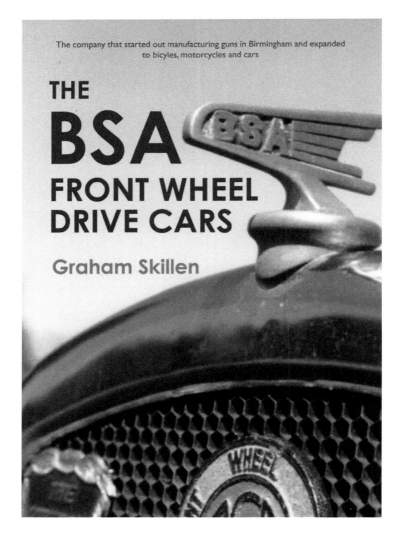

The BSA Front Wheel Drive Cars

Graham Skillen

The first book about the ground-breaking BSA front wheel drive cars.

978-1-4456-5371-6

96 pages, illustrated throughout

The History of the Sunbeam Alpine

John Willshire

The full history of the Sunbeam Alpine, including its design and racing history.

978-1-4456-4758-6
96 pages, illustrated throughout

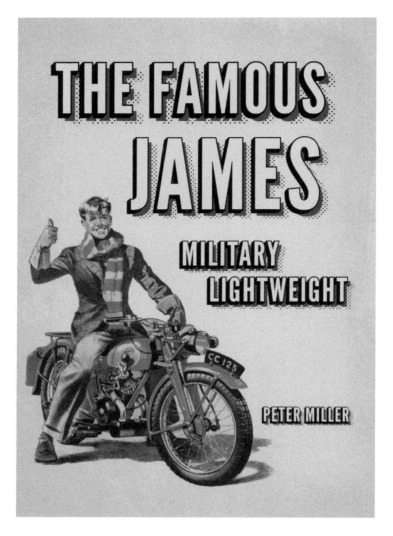